PRAYERFUL PAUSES WITH JESUS AND MARY

PRAYERFUL PAUSES

WITH

JESUS AND MARY

WILLIAM PEFFLEY

TWENTY-THIRD PUBLICATIONS

Mystic, Connecticut

Cover photo credit: The Station "Jesus Meets His Mother" was sculptured by Arthur Dooley of Liverpool, England, for the Church of St. Mary in Leyland Lancashire, England. It was photographed by Michael Brooks and Richard Mahoney for the slide/tape presentation "The Way to Calvary" by Sound-in-Focus, Ltd. Used with SIF permission.

Twenty-Third Publications
P.O. Box 180
Mystic CT 06355
(203) 536-2611

Library of Congress Catalog Card Number 85-50690
ISBN 0-89622-251-9

Edited and designed by John G. van Bemmel

CONTENTS

JOY

SORROW

TRIUMPH

GLORY

INTRODUCTION

The cycle of joy, sorrow, and triumph stands like a three-fingered signpost at the crossroads of human life, and we are all bound to travel those directions at one time or another.

Sometimes it's a gradual journey as when one passes from the joy of *presence* to the sorrow of a loved one lost, to the triumph of acceptance and hope. At other times there is a merging of emotion; the saints, for example, found within their pain a certain joy, even triumph in the depths of their sorrow.

This three-pronged experience reached its perfection in the lives of Jesus and Mary where joy, sorrow, and triumph are shown as God would live them, as God indeed did live them. Now they are set forever like three brilliant stars in the sky of human existence, full of Christian promise, signaling the galaxy of glory that sails beyond.

This little book presents a few New Testament events to serve as wayside shrines, spots to rest along the road, occasions to pause beside the signpost and contemplate the stars.

JOY

THE GIFTS

*A virgin betrothed
to a man named Joseph
of the House of David*   Luke 1:27

A staff of oak he'd given
carved symbol of a strength
pledge of dedication
for all her yielded length of days;

some chips of cedar in a pouch
fragrant sign
of love as old as Lebanon
and as enduring;

a polished cube of ebony
for her to hold
enfold
in hand —
keepsake of his unworthiness. . .

For him:

her smile
like melody in still strings;

her crystal days
threaded through with silver vow;

her form at prayer
teaching him new silences
driving into him new strengths
like pegs into beams . . . .

THE MOMENT

A town in Galilee
called Nazareth   Luke 1:26

Perhaps a garden
some still corner of a room
rooftop breezeless under stars
a step in sleep . . .

Solitude there surely was
and silence —
soundlessness
like deep hollows of unentered caves
or languid settling of dust on summer roads;

a quiet time
perhaps afternoon
windowed by long slant of sun
when slightest
shadowed
sliver of a leaf
attracts attention

or twilight
when wafted voices round the busy well
seep into distant hills
and prayer
like dusk descending

deepens . . . .

THE MESSENGER

The angel Gabriel
was sent by God   Luke 1:26

With a look like lightning
and a storm for wings
he sped toward earth
in that first of Springs!

Powers bent backward
and Dominions fell
at the timed explosion
in his seraph-shell!

O the world had waited
had waited long
and the world grew weary
of the waiting song . . . .

THE ENCOUNTER

*He went in
and said to Mary
Rejoice*   Luke 1:28

Did she know him as a fragrance by her side
exquisite as eternal things might be
and there in inward swoon
breathe her willingness to love?

Was he giant to the mind
immense
intense in imagery

or was he for the moment
man
messengered and mighty
as scriptures often tell?

Or light —
perhaps he came as light:

mere dots at first
pinpricks in the drape of darkness
hung behind closed childhood eyes
until —
light-pierced
threadbare —
the perforated fabric fell
and light itself became a veil
more blinding than the dark!

THE QUESTION

*Mary asked herself
what this greeting could mean*   Luke 1:30

Had they met before
these two creations
singular and vast?

He
timeless
spaceless
world unto himself
God-made medium
for the God-Man mystery;

she
planetized
rooted in a people and a place —
clear vein of diamond
in a mine-scarred earth:

had they met before?

She almost nonchalantly
accepts his visitation
more concerned with words
than other-worldly being
making meaning certain
in this sudden thrust upon her understanding . . .

She must have known him
long and very well
to have entrusted him
with that astounding

Yes.

THE CHOICE

I am the handmaid
of the Lord   Luke 1:37

There was a dawn, a certain tree
bird, antelope and bee
and things were green.

And there was noon; throughout the glade
lay a calm God had made
and God was seen.

Then something stirred within the leaves
there came a moment — it was Eve's:
small creatures ran!

Dusk turned to night. Nothing slept.
Off a branch a serpent crept . . .
And there hid Man.

Unlike Eve
this gleaming Judith-blade
drawn from out our scabbard time
cleaved the serpent's branch
pruned the tree of pestilence
and drew Life's latent liquor
from its root!

THE DECISION

*Let what you have said
be done to me*   Luke 1:38

Is it true we owe her everything?

Has all poverty gone
by this one mere turning
of her glass and flawless key
ancient vault flung open
stocked for our looting?

Had she said *no*
how would He have come?
What Divine Alternative
would have been pressured from that Maker-Mind
had this once and only woman
willed a different way?

No matter now
nor then —
for age on age
and age to come
receives this Gift of her

who embryoed *Eternal*
who infanted the Infinite.

THE FULFILLMENT

You are to conceive
and bear a son   Luke 1:32

Long had she watched him come:

a speck on her horizoned heart
a tiny barque against the skies of Yahwehed years
a vessel veering
veering toward her
as to some longed-for charted port . . .

Along her mind's white shore
waves of psalm and prophet broke

currents
fresh and hidden
wore away the pilings of all doubt
until
behind her reef of will —
in angel-squall! —
he finds his chaste and custom cove!

Nestled now in oval ark
still and soundless inlet sealed
he rides earth's rhythm-rippled tide
moored to gentle harbor.

THE SILENCE

*She was found
to be with child*   Matthew 1:18

To tell of God
is not an easy thing —
though He be thunder in the heart!

Lines that wait their balance on the tongue
to structure His Magnificence
must ever be but scaffold for His praise:

for words are flesh
through which the soul
must bleed its flood
droplets at a time

and thoughts are birds
trapped
in narrow towers
with all the distance of a sky
aching in their wings . . .

The Anguish

*Her husband Joseph
being a man of honor
and wanting to spare her publicity
decided to divorce her informally*   Matthew 1:19

I look to you
across the things man cannot say
across a chasmed moment
canyon-deep
to learn the distance of a lover's gaze
to gauge the depth of meaning
beneath a tongue of stone . . .

What heart is there can bridge
what silence canopy this void
where faith must carve a jagged line
and wear a distant wordless language
off the lonely banks of time . . . .

THE LOSS

*He had made up his mind
to do this*   Matthew 1:20

A deep majestic wing
snuffs out the sun;

some smothered fumes of gold
and day is done:

and now there leans a wing
upon my heart

with all the weight of two
in love

apart . . . .

13

THE REJOICING

*The angel of the Lord
appeared to him in a dream and said
Do not be afraid
to take Mary home as your wife*   Matthew 1:20

Now I know
there is no end to song
though instrument should warp
and voice crumble
with the final dust of sound!

Should my sun swallow its light
and all the galaxies go dead
inside my dark

should there be no more roads
no fields of destiny to run
Beloved!
there would still be song!

Now I know
I'll travel all the roads with you
and spend my light
singing!

THE JOURNEY

Mary set out at that time
and went as quickly as she could
to a town
in the hill country of Judah   Luke 1:39

Now is she old enough
to learn that certain journeys
are signs of human seasons as they pass

to sense the normal days are gone —
meadow-days
days of childhood dream
and undemanding dance —

days like sandprints
trailing in her teenage wake
tracking
softly tracking
the widening path of destiny:

for this is the desert edge
coveted clearing
last homeward path of promise
her people are to know!

Now is she older than the sea
bearing all its life;
wiser than the sky
absorbing all its suns . . .

Like fragrant rush of april air
she skirts familiar hills
punctuating clouds with psalm
fencing mile on awe-filled mile
with canticle!

THE VESSEL

Elizabeth
whom people called barren
is now in her sixth month　　Luke 1:36

Out of this desert-womb
a spring appeared
up-bubbled from buried prophet-flow
silent running
of an old and shallowing stream . . .

Had she felt its hidden current
through the long years of drought
or known there moved within her
its final rivulet
racing toward the ritual of Grace?

She would be an earthen dish for cleansing —
a shell
from which the first ablutions
would pour upon the forehead of the world!

THE MEETING

*Mary went into Zechariah's house
and greeted Elizabeth*   Luke 1:40

Like met meadows
these two become a boundary of praise:
hopes hedgerow
testaments entwine
and lace with psalmody!

One
once barren field
now roots a desert shrub
solitary
strong
reaching for the howl of future winds
to sound along its branches
like a mighty herald-horn;

the other
young oasis
spears forth her first of vineyard yield
a Wonder-Shoot
encasing grace
and multi-fruited sacrament . . .

Parallel along this ancient line
like two columns of a saplinged arch
they touch —
wind-thatch —
in holy gust of joy!

THE GREETING

The moment your greeting
reached my ears
the child in my womb
leaped for joy   Luke 1:44

She had gone unnoticed
a changeless contour of the countryside
familiar as worn flagstones
by the village well;
townsfolk
long ago
had lain aside her motherhood
like an empty sheepskin pouch
dry
brittle in disuse . . .

O seasoned sheath for prophet-blade
clasped now to Judah's belt!
Heirloomed scabbard
for Yahweh's desert steel!
You peer into your cousins's jewel youth
as through a goblet brimmed with wine
to find a kingdom in this cup
a Conquerer
so quiet in his coming
so gentle in his war
you sing of joyful stabbing
as he
within you reaching
already wields your tiny sword!

THE SIEGE

Joseph set out
from the town of Nazareth in Galilee
and traveled up to Judea
to the town of David
called Bethlehem   Luke 2:4

The Warrior-King approaches:
encased in her inviolate mail
wrapped in linen armor
behind a blanket shield
on drab and donkey steed
weaponless
he takes the city!

Cave-encamped
star-banner raised
proclamation posted on the angel-side of sky —
thus ends his secret siege . . .

Soon from his victor-chamber he'll appear
to claim a livestock court
a conquered race of two
and there
mid shepherd spoils
in triumph troughed
will accept his throne . . .

And when he sleeps
along his limp and infant arm
she'll lay a scepter-strand of straw

THE TREE

Joseph
the husband of Mary
of her was born Jesus
who is called Christ   Matthew 1:16

Like a tree was he to grow
this mustard seed:

cypress through the Herod marsh
wall of oak in exile
pomegranate for the grove of Galilee.

His touch for her was always willow
his thought a cedar-scent . . .

And now his firm and weathered limb
nests her exotic Bird
earth-flung and vulnerable
stowed in his shade!

THE CROWN

The sight of the star
filled the wise men with delight
and going into the house
they saw the Child
with his mother Mary   Matthew 2:11

She who was to shake stars from her veil
in some apocalyptic time to come
had no need for hint of royalty
for star-crowns set above her dwelling:
here
asleep
epitome of Kings!

We have seen his star in the east

His star:
for him
too young to rule
to claim predestinate dominion
she was his every boundary
his one and total kingdom;

hence gold and scented gifts received
accepted by her hands

His gifts
her hands . . .

What of questions asked
stories told
his story
glowing through her starlight voice?

(Her words
his story
her voice
his *Word!*)

The marvelling
long moments of the studied heart
a meal
and finally farewell . . .

*They had seen his star in the east
and had come to worship him*

His star
her crown.

THE PATH

*They took him
up to Jerusalem
to present him to the Lord* Luke 2:22

Forty days of fatherness
and now once more the road;

her road —
he was to know it well:
like worked wood
or gentle goodness
it was always to be his

(not so the dreams —
dreams were meant to be but worn
to crack like faded leather aprons
discarded in one's course of toil)

Like lines upon a scroll of plans
connecting all the master-points
her paths were sure for him
trusted means to work a Will's design . . .

He scanned them now
and traced this temple-turn of road —
beyond he could not read.

But his were willing pilgrim feet
and hers the only path.

THE RANSOM

To offer in sacrifice
a pair of turtledoves   Luke 2:24

To ransom a Redeemer
the price was paid in doves:
soft throb of wing
hidden in extended hands
spasmed signal for a sacrifice
the holy burning
that bought her first-born back . . .

This day would smolder on her heart
like incense fume through shielded years
until another day of ransom
when on Redemption's pyre
she will have placed her only Dove
and stood beneath his spread still wings
to wait the end of emberings.

THE SWORD

And a sword will pierce
your own soul too   Luke 2:34, 35

The unseen blade of torment
(already in her girlhood tightly lodged)
the old man twists:

its herod-hilt she'll ponder
its eve's-edge long endure
til forged to final form
in Roman steel
it spears a Victim's side . . .

Then she
no stranger to that thrust
still living
will have died.

THE FAMILY

Every year
his parents used to go
to Jerusalem   Luke 2:41

Like bits of parchment
stored in cosmic jars
mere incidents are found
that tell of cave
or temple-step
or village road;

what of their scroll of years
lettered in that *One Word* tongue
paragraphed by that one man and wife?

What of their days
their days
their *everydays*
maps of moments
telling and detailed
heart-sketched
autographed
diaries of Divinity?

Deciphered fragments of some feast
quaint custom
or some daily chore —
all these the mind enthrall:

but O to *know* those three dim figures
on time's faded ancient wall!

THE SEARCH

The boy Jesus stayed behind
without his parents knowing it   Luke 2:43

In years to come
she'll search through crowds again
scan multitudes for sight of him
and there
mid other Temple minds
hear further of a *Father*
and questions for her pondering:
Who is my mother?

Through some three future days —
another journey to Jerusalem achieved —
she'll suffer loss
when night begins at noon
when Sabbath is his hiding place
when entrance to the Temple is a tomb . . .

Then a man will come
who like her husband now
will hold her close
wrap his life about her
and take her home.

THE FINDING

They found him in the Temple
sitting among the Doctors
listening to them
and asking them questions   Luke 2:46

The elders hint of harvest for his mind:

he forages their learning
tugs their wisdom-roots
like an apprenticed gardener
avid for growth.

Her Simeoned seed
sprung shoot of Temple soil
takes in ancient air
draws moisture from the sacred stream
and finds his rooting
in his *Father's place.*

THE FATHER

See how worried
your father and I have been
looking for you . . .
Did you not know
that I must be busy
with my Father's affairs?   Luke 2:48, 49

With a hip-side bag of tools
and a boy hugged to his back —
joyfully apprenticed! —
he had climbed the scaffold
of those childhood years;

now
from these three rungs of anxious days
from this level Temple-high
he views the rooftops of the past
and there
ahead
the distant ending of the road:

he knows the boy must now come down a man
the boy who's found tools of his own
and new Apprenticeship:
one father's boy —
another Father's Son . . .

Turning to descend
he finds
again
a youngster's hand in his:
firmly
like some warm and waxen seal
it takes the total impress
of all this father's years.

THE SHAWL

*Jesus went down with them
and came to Nazareth
and lived under their authority*   Luke 2:51

Trust:

she draws it close about her
like a shawl;

a shawl
tinged with anguish
tassled with awe

a shawl to hold as veil
between the God-glare and her sight
diffusion for each new dawn's Divinity;

a shawl to serve as shroud one day
when
caught on thorn
torn by nail
blood-drenched and hung by spear
she'll wrap him in it
God-side-out
and bury him that way . . . .

SORROW

THE GARDEN

*There was a garden there
and Jesus went into it
with his disciples*   John 18:1

A rock to prop an arm upon;

black sky
horizonless;

shrubs like frightened animals
cowered in dark;

no sound . . .

no sound but hiss of slithered stream
gasp of intermittent breeze
men in rustled slumber
out of sight;

no sound —

no sound except this hammered horror
willed upon an anviled Heart
sending rings
Redeemed
Redeemed
down the distant valleys of the years!

MEMORIES

If it is possible
let this cup pass me by   Matthew 26:39

Childhood mornings
bright with village play . . .

writhing shadows
on the somber brook

master-feel of crafted wood
on waning quiet afternoons . . .

slow disciples
helpless —
clustering dusk

earth-scented evenings
nazarethed
serene . . .

blades of cloud
piercing the sun
in skies the color of pain.

THE CONSOLER

Then an angel appeared to Jesus
coming from heaven
to give him strength   Luke 22:43

Long dis-paradised
God's edened man returns;

the ancient proposition
like a millstone
massive
moving
crushes him to earth:

where once a temptor coiled —
its dark gifts
sheathed in weakness
scaled with shame —
there stands a bright consoler
sworded sentry of the garden gate
who welcomes him . . .

O what outcome of this night:
an angel's flaming sword dies out
and with it all the age-old need
for guarding paradise!

THE TESTING

Sadness came over him
and great distress   Matthew 26:37

Here pain's deluge
crested once for all:
prostrate in his flesh-built ark
frightened doves released
(O let it pass!)
he waits submissive
for their bright return . . .

There will be rainbows down the sky
Brilliance at the dawn!

But not for now:

for now
the slump of shouldered centuries
years-worn words of weakness
uttered by mankind one final time
(O let it pass!)

for now
darkness —
darkness
and sudden dread:
bobbing torches on a garden road . . .

No dove returns

The latch at last is sprung:
our Noah sets his foot
upon a sodden earth.

THE DEFENSE

Lord they said
there are two swords here
He said to them
that is enough   Luke 22:38

Two swords

unthreatable weapons
tin blades
for chopping childhood air
at make-believe marauders
on some golden plain of glory;

two swords

naive protection
for all mankind's security —
rustable defense
for sheer Omnipotence!

THE CLOWN

*The men who had arrested Jesus
led him off*   Matthew 26:57

There was another night
when inns of insignificance
refused his entourage
clamed no room for royalty
no space for hidden splendor.

Now they all must have him:

darkened domicile of priests
insists he play
recite his lines
through long and heckled hours;

castle of a cardboard king
demands a magic of him
its shackled clown;

fortress of a governor
foregoes all tricks for truth
and tests its silent seer
with tense soliloquy . . .

Dangled thus from stage to stage
by bands of drunken puppeteers
in costume for finale
he takes insane applause!

THE CONCERT

Some of them started spitting at him
and blindfolding him
began hitting him with their fists
and shouting Play the prophet!   Mark 14:65

The toying of demented children
with Love's priceless violin:

strung
plucked
struck

their dirge is played upon him

decadent discordant prelude
to sin's masterwork . . . .

THE RITE

Then Herod together with his guards
treated him with contempt
and made fun of him
he put a rich cloak on him
and sent him back to Pilate   Luke 23:11

Ceremonial servants
aides to paradox of rite:
theirs the sad perverted privilege
to mishandle Heavenwear
to vest with desecration
crown with gargoyled glee
this inverse king!

For *not a sparrow falls*
nor raucous soldier hails
nor fisted reed descends
that is not clue to Love's refraction
key to providential code:

jeers —
inverted tribute;

insult —
converse praise;

pain —
coin of a peaceful realm
received of subjects
loved in their lunacy
blessed in their sordid sacrament!

LAWS

You would have no power over me
replied Jesus
if it had not been given you
from above   John 19:11

Here no laws are miracled
except for one:
the potter has become a jar
the artist his own handiwork
the maker his material;

hence feet fastened will not dance
pain-closed eyes not glow
nor mystery shield
thwart a threatening crowd:

bones obey the press of wood
flesh the singe of whip
and God
the gravity . . . .

THE DETOUR

They had Jesus taken away
and scourged   John 19:1

Why this jaunt of taunters
unnecessary detour
off paschal road
road obvious and open
inevitably to be travelled?
Temple victims are never led to torture —
swift thrust of priestly hand
and all is done.

Not here —
here gray shepherds
roam a pavement pasture
with their flock of One;

laughter
like an obscene horn
blares through the watchless night
as the Lamb is shackled
shorn
seared alive
upon a granite spit!

Then the road again
just as before . . .

Why this jarring journey
off Redemption's routed way?

Flesh dyes a crimson answer
into the pain-splotched cloak
while all inconsequential cravings
clot
upon the Lamb-King's skin . . . .

THE PRINCE

Having twisted some thorns
into a crown
they put it on his head
and placed a reed in his right hand

Matthew 27:29

There was a mangered moment
(when he was Prince of Peace)
wood was soft with straw
linen-lined and low
in reach of simple servants.

Wood there was once more
(when he was Prince of Paradise)
erected high on quarried dais
rigid down his blood-caped back
along torn outreach of arm
beneath the steel-slit foot.

A stump of marble now
chipped soldier-stool perhaps
or splattered granite bench
where prisoners had rested
between dying and death:

here
cloaked for comedy
in burred and berried cap
the Prince of Pain performs
impersonates Himself . . . .

THE SYMBOL

To make fun of him
they knelt to him saying
Hail king of the Jews!   Matthew 27:29

Was this unholy gathering
the first demonic mockery of Man —
god-aspirant Man —
spirit-sprung toward angel realm
and now perhaps beyond?

Had long satanic testing
found the perfect specimen
the satisfying equal to a deadly jest?

A would-be king
power like their own
enigmatic energy
tinged with tantalizing weakness!
(His strength was known by desert trial
his frailty from Pilate's pillared pause . . .)

Hence *thorn and cloak*
and sceptered joke
and bloody body battering!

To no avail
though men had died from scourging many times:
no anti-symbol here
no cold and hard-cut column
to stand as sign for near-redemption
to mark earth's ages
with a chiseled "I" of stone —
memorial to God's manacled Mistake!

For wood had waited
warm upon the earth
limbed
leafed
pliant in purpose:
seasoned
shaped
and crafted crossed
to fit the height of Holocaust

THE OBSERVER

Here is the man   John 19:6

She could have been among
the crowd that heard those words
Behold the man!

She could have seen
in stained unravelled remnant of a son
the seamless star-stiched robe of glory

and in the gruesome trappings of the trial
charaded plan
controlled maneuver of a mighty Love:

for *all* her seeing
had been optical illusion
design of bi-reality
providential paradox of sight:
virginity —
yet motherhood;
human child —
yet Personed God;
death inevitable —
yet ever Life . . .

Though faith exists to see
when mind can see no longer
what of sight
when *faith* can see no more?

Crucified
let him be crucified! . . .

Thus could have stood this blind observer
now turning toward her ultimate horizon
seeking light's last vestige
prior to all dark

she whose irridescent womanhood
once wove the fabric of a man
to serve as garment for the vagrancy of God.

The Trail

*Carrying his own cross
he went out of the city*   John 19:17

Once there had been time
for roaming rare plateaus
for lingering on ledges
overlooking life
his words like sun-tinged air
upon their up-turned hearts.

Smooth had been the rising road
mountain-wide
with snow-sheen prophets at its peak!

Whence descent?
Whence the narrow garden path
nettled joys
hopes crouched in overgrowth
love sharp and stoney underfoot?

A trail remained
no wider than a builder's beam
cut through a human forest
with room for only

One.

THE PLANTING

If men use the green wood
like this
what will happen
when it is dry?   Luke 23:31

Like an oozing bough
unseasoned for saw-cut
they graft him to a splintered log
lashing deep graffiti
into his tender bark;

they trim the women from him
beat back the hedgerow hands
and clear a site for planting . . .

By noon the vineyard's done
and he is slung
our Vine
on trellised wing
braced and pruned
for blossoming.

The Followers

Then all the disciples
deserted him
and ran away   Matthew 26:56

Where are the followers
through this
the climax of their calling?

Nine
like fish darting —
startled in their placid depth
by plunging terror-weight —
shadow-hide;

one
root-severed vine
like a slowing pendulum
swings stiff and silent
from a breeze-brushed branch;

one
earth-sunk rock
split by Staff-strike
spills a reservoir of tears!

PRAYER OF JUDAS

When he found
that Jesus had been condemned
Judas His betrayer was filled with remorse

Matthew 27:3

The gargoyle crumbles
at the fount of my will
O King of the Flaming Law!
Your blade has split
its whale-lipped frown
that spewed deceit
like hailstones at your fire-feet
and hated your advancing heat!

Now tower walls are seared
self heaves your name from lungs of smoke
and all my charred belongings
ember-burst
smolder at your heel
cursed . . .

So come
fling your spear of final burning on my cold debris
O Lover of the Lava Heart!
and let my last gnarled cedar
carbon at your touch of suns!

Then breathe —
perhaps —
my ashes to your winds
as of a thing once blessed and burned
sacramental
worn
older than my sins . . . .

PRAYER OF PETER

Peter remembered . . .
and he went outside
and wept bitterly   Luke 22:61-62

I saw your image O God of Light
yet eyes were stones
prayer was slate behind my brow
gray apprehension chilled my bones;

waiting my gaze to crack like clay upon your splendor
my heart was ore
wedged in wooden flesh —
mossed
stifled
every pore.

But now
now my heart is running molten
from the furnace of your hand
sorrow fumes like scented bark
under faith's ignited brand

bones are benedictions
smoldering like years
and O my eyes
my granite eyes
spill their miracle of tears!

THE STORM

The people stayed there
watching him . . .
As for the leaders
they jeered at him   Luke 23:35

Lightly falls the scarlet rain!
sing the many leak-proof hearts
ring the tiny love-proof huts
under hidden lightning chains.

Lovely flows the scarlet stream!
mime the soft submerging isles
chime the shrill vermillion bells
while the unheard thunder screams.

The Storm
The Storm
is purple-veined
a swollen sky of longing;

the rent horizon
drains itself
of stars
and stars

THE BEGGAR

Jesus knew
that everything had now been completed
and to fulfill the scripture perfectly
he said
I am thirsty   John 19:28

A beggar languishes of thirst
beside the wells of human wills
his eyes aware of every drop
a drunken human nature spills

from its clay cup . . . he sees the crowd
the futile dips into desire
that scooping-up of quenchlessness
the frantic gulps, the dregs of fire:

what worth a beggar's plea I thirst!
to self-intoxicated hearts?
where find 'samaritans' who ask
that thirsting end — while *Thirsting* starts?

A bloated world would drown its life
at satisfaction's stagnant brink
while Living Water languishes
and vainly pleads: Give me a drink! . . .

THE DOE

Near the cross of Jesus
stood his mother   John 19:25

A cage of crowd
hems her in;

gaze
gawk
goad
all thrash about her:

stung —
compassion's cheek

torn —
her sorrow's veil . . .

Alert and still
deep in her forest of pain
she stands

like a doe in some familiar thicket
a hind in her own habitat.

The Loved One

Seeing his mother
and the disciple he loved standing near her
he said to John
This is your mother   John 1:26

I find no beauty in your face O God
of loveliness! From sight of you I reel —
poor total wound! Your passion sighs from sod
soaked with your blood (O waste of Love's appeal —

like crimson honey poured for flies!) I feign
disciple-stance, but fear wears fragile masks
and I can now no longer hide the strain
of matching love for *Love* — nor face the tasks!

I have been lover of an unblotched brow:
(no sweat, no clot, no spittle to erase!)
unlike this woman pain-wed with you now
my kiss is eager for your *easter* face!

So sorrow comes — Love's single sweet rebuff —
the sorrow that no sorrow is enough . . . .

THE FRUIT

Woman
this is your son

It is accomplished   John 19:26-30

Staying the demanded distance
like a still dove in wind-walled cote
she eyes the tri-stemmed stalk
(grotesque atop its mound of skull)
and moans to wing its violet height
to dye her breast the color of its leaves
to nest within the petals of its pain . . .

Soon
stirred by paschal rain
her great garnet Bud
burgeons
blooms
and sags
with sudden yield . . . .

No longing now
no flight —

only nesting
nesting
in the hollow of his side
like a mauve blossom
on an indigo tree. . . .

TRIUMPH

THE WITNESS

It was very early
and still dark
when Mary of Magdala
came to the tomb   John 20:1

A brittle glaze of night
encrusts the grove.

Nothing moves.

Soon a timid insect
advertises dawn —

footsteps then
footsteps chipping silence off a path:
they tack a presence to the trees
and quake the valley
with their echoing haste!

She comes;

reckless in her need
fearless in her simple love
tomb-bound
she comes:

first
envied
eager witness
to this

our Sacred Vacancy!

THE VISITORS

Two men
in brilliant clothes
suddenly appeared at their side   Luke 24:4

This they had never seen:
young men dressed in sky!
The women only know to fear
to fall upon the fresh-hewn stone
frenzied
dumb
like altar victims
readied for the temple knife.

But there will be no knives
for this is the Gentle Time
when blades must twist to plowshares
and terror melt in shining tears of joy!

Face down in garment pools
submerged
their senses drown . . .

Soon the stillness
like an ocean deep and unperturbed
floats them to the surface of the mind:

No Lord
There was *no Lord* . . .
Risen as He said!

They spring like specters from the empty tomb
and race the sunrise to the city walls!

THE BELIEVERS

This story of theirs
seemed pure nonsense
and they did not believe them   Luke 24:11

Cries crack the dome of morning;
hands play doors like frantic drums

but no urgency can bridge their deep abyss
no women's shimmering words
plumb this well of sorrow!

Of course they saw Him —
won't anyone who ever saw Him
forever see Him?
This was reality:
a dead man buried
steel to beam
blood to earth
flesh to slab
reality!

No chance now to trace the terror-road
and at each bend
defend
with sword and gallant glance:
for love lay lame
self-wounded far from battle
fallen on its own blunt blade
routed at mere rooster-cry!

The women's pleas
(escape-ropes for a grasping faith)
splash within reach of consciousness:

clutched at last
tested
they hold —
bearing up the weight of fishermen!

THE AVALANCHE

Then at last
he appeared to all eleven   Mark 16:14

Yes, it is true
The Lord has risen
and has appeared to Simon   Luke 24:34

Huddled on their hidden ridge of history
they hear the resurrection stories
crash like boulders down the mountain-week:

Had they too not felt the rumblings
from his varied peaks of miracle
heard first-hand his words
now strewn like fallen shards
about the base of memory?
Was faith to ever be a climber
clinging where no foothold can be found
hugging
helpless
hopeless
slopes of the impossible
in path of certain Avalanche?

The make-shift shelter
niche to settle in
to while away the mysteries
around self's puny fire
is not for these:

now
the first of them
crushed by wonder
caved by Love
reels down this new reality
tumbling ten plus tens of millions
with him
to their Life!

THE VESTMENT

Then he took them out
as far as the outskirts of Bethany   Luke 24:50

This foothill of eternity
they clothe as with an alb
vesting their Master
with a stole of humble stance.

Never will they know the lands
their hem
disciple-deep
will touch

nor for what future liturgy
they weave this vestment-praise;

but in this second *lifting up*
there shines bright presage of a Third
when they become his blessing hands
to multiply his Wafer-Word
to raise his resurrection-Cup
in timeless toast
to Total Love!

Upon the back of Bethany there lays
a people-patterned cloak —
its shoulder now is worship-slung
while clouds
like incense
filigree in Glory.

THE CLIMAX

They asked him
Lord, has the time come?
Are you going to restore
the kingdom of Israel?   Acts 1:6

So near the journey's end!
One slight and final climb
and they'll have reached the apex of their world!

Below them and beyond
like the distant studded valley
lay all the happenings:
they'd passed
like Jonah
through the city's breadth
through those *three days* and more
proclaiming to each other
the coming and the glory of this time!

Now it was on to home —
and *Him!*
Off the high horizon soon He'll stride
and all upon this mount
will fade into the Fatherdom
promised and prepared!

But whence this spoken lightning
out the placid sky:
You will be witnesses!
fire fingering the mind:
to the ends
to the ends of the earth!

There is worship now
upward straining after sky
wonder
puzzled weeping
slow descent . . . .

THE HOPE

*Now as he blessed them
he withdrew from them*　　Luke 24:51

Unknowingly they'd climbed
those harvest-hearted
a springtime slope:

to them it was the season
for threshing of dreams
long-looked-for goods-gathering
fill of feasting;

time when daily winds
no longer chilled their jostling buds of joy
and peace
at last
relaxed its cautious tendrils
set to grip the shale of certain loss . . .

Now skies are weatherless;
all past is petal
out-turned and torn in sudden air
wrenched at stem-point
sweet Climate of their rooting gone
with all the seasons of their guarded growth!

Long do they linger
on the time-numb hill
offering an orchard
of dumb-founded praise . . .

But there
along tomorrow's rim
a massive Storm of Joy
with rain to ravish every root
to blossom every limb
to inundate the earth with fruit
and blaze the world with Him
with Him!

PONDERINGS

And so the Lord Jesus
was taken up into heaven Mark 16:19

Gone from her sight was he
many times before:

just days from birth
his immediate immersion
in cloth font of aging arms
that left her damp with prophecy
as she received him back;

at twelve
his brief eclipse
blinding
as it caught her unprotected gaze
fixed upon his Temple flare;

those public years
with dense and endless fence of crowd
that gave but slotted glimpses
as he passed;

the stone
the stone
shouldered into place
that turned her cradle-heart to crypt!

And now
the clouds
like swaddling clothes
folding him from sight . . . .

ASCENSION NIGHT

*So from the Mount of Olives
they went back to Jerusalem*   Acts 1:12

Tell me Mary what you see
staring out towards Galilee:

*Eyes can see so far at times
so far at times.*

Lady what is it you hear
as you listen there and peer?

*Earth can be so still at times
so still at times.*

Mother tell me what you feel
why you turn and slowly kneel!

*Child our joy is sad at times
so sad at times.*

THE THRONE

And know that I am with you
always   Matthew 28:20

They view her fondly
as some cherished heirloom left behind
carved with his likeness
embellished with remembrance of his touch.

Hidden once within her cushioned hollow
he lounged his time toward light;

poised upon her years ago
he took the triuned tribute of the East;

resting in her firm and velvet ways
(O Chair of Christendom!)
he readied for a kingdom thirty years.

And she was throne once more
when tattered shroud of kingly flesh
was draped across her regal arms . . . .

Empty now
majestic in stillness
she alone expects the visit of the Wind
fire-form of Wisdom
who comes to stay
to rule
to occupy his throne.

THE WAITING

When they reached the city
they went to the upper room
where they were staying   Acts 1:13

What will happen
when the silence ends
when walls no longer seal the city out
and life once more remembers us?

Or will the silence end?

Does the day come when no day comes
when we are left to stare forever
toward our vacant sky?

Waiting has the roots of years
a mine of longing lines our depths;
wine that ran our veins with sun
and burst us into blossoming
has frozen to our bones —

joys that swooped the distance
from our senses to our soul like doves
today are bats with olive twigs
diving on our hearts!

THE PRAYING

All these joined in continuous prayer
together with several women
including Mary
the mother of Jesus   Acts 1:14

The Mother sits
a silence within the silence.

She wears her waiting like a hood.

They watch her peer
beyond the length of seeing
know she listens
to the inner side of sound.

They range around her prayer like shrubs
and reach their hopes to her like branches.

Moments filter
drop by drop
into the room . . .

Then
along the soul's edge
a Tone begins
hearts are reeds quivered —
woodwinds for exquisite Breath

and bodies bow
in feared seared surprise
beneath cantatas of a Wind!

THE TREASURE

*When Pentecost day came round
they had all met in one room*   Acts 2:1

*One other room had she prepared for him
it too once filled with fire:
nine months the molten melody
set within her furnaced form
was cast to her perfection
then solar-like leapt to breath
and cooled to touch in Bethlehem.*

They group for gleaning
a barren mine of prayer.

She waits with them
diamonding their dark;
bids them scale
faith's untested crevice
dark slag-sides of doubt
to reach the treasure-vein —
Love's living layer
burning unconsumably
immense and incomputable!

There comes a shifting in the caverned quiet
rumbling near the wind-cleft heart
pelting of divine debris
of ecstasy!

They leap to her in laughter
drop drunkenly to kneel
to reel
in wonder of it all!

Then
gathering their fortune
flee —
flinging it to multitudes!

The Beginning

*And they were all filled
with the Holy Spirit*   Acts 2:4

Fresh being hums
drums
thunders down our dark:

private earths quake
and all our troubled seas
slip from the surface of the soul!

Day is our garment
our cincture flame;
seasons for sandals
speech like sky
(golden gospel teeming from tongues!)

we sing our making with tomorrow's voice
and tilt the mountains
with a mustard seed!

GLORY

THE SEED

Whatever you sow in the ground
has to die
before it is given new life
and the thing you sow
is not what is going to come   1 Corinthians 15:36

This seed was sown
to spear our bouldered time
to thrive in death's deep crag
to spring like fern
from clay and shaley soil.

Our seedling laws —
root
to shoot
to bloom
to reed
to seed again —
no more apply:

transplanted now
gardened in Ever-Spring
sole sprig of species long extinct
in Him we grow
sun-bent and beautiful
towards the harvest of our dreams!

FIRST FRUIT

*Christ has in fact been raised from the dead
the first fruits of all
who have fallen asleep*   1 Corinthians 15:20

Her *first fruit*
once Presented
dove-redeemed
returned to her
when lanes were lined with innocence.

Her *first fruit*
unripened
lost in tangled days of trust
returned to her
when paths were paved with peace.

Her *first fruit*
harvested
a damaged husk of flesh
returned to her
when roads were ridged with pain.

Her *first fruit*
wheat-wrapped
grape-hid
meal of miracle
returned to her
when ways were still with joy.

Her *first fruit*
glory-garbed
returned to her
touching to wholeness
lifting to totality
ending all the roads!

BUTTERFLY

If in union with Christ
we have imitated his death
we shall also imitate him
in his resurrection   Romans 6:5

This butterfly
knew no cocoon
no phase of worm
in wrapped oblivion:
winged beauty always
to Beauty
winged
was drawn.

ENDINGS

After I have gone
and prepared you a place
I shall return to take you with me   John 14:3

All endings are beginnings:

fade of day begins the night
the edge of sea the shore;
starting points
of drawn lines closed
begin a ring's infinity.

So dusk is she
sole glow of our diminished day
first sign of star-time
past our sun-shed hills;

tide is she
first wave to kiss our destined coast
to spray our homeland sand;

tie is she
knot for our race's severed cord
weld of our yearning's
long-broken chain!

THE CURE

I have given them the glory
you gave to me   John 17:22

Though she was cure for Eve's malaise
no crypt could store her
like some urned elixir
against contaminated days to come:

her vault was shattered like a water jar
and she
pure gush of cana spring
wined now to golden newness
draws us
in her sparkling flow!

THE DRAGON

*The great dragon
who had deceived all the world
was hurled down to the earth*   Revelation 12:9

A gangrenous being
long dis-seraphimed
mocks our mingling with the virgin-wine:
its ancient waste has fouled our well
till stagnance lizards through our veins
and there is lust for mildew
on our brand new tongues!

It screams at sanctity's clean bed
with cess-soul sighs would vomit *Bread* . . .

But there's a bride
a star-pure bride
virgin omnipregnant
smiling down our day:
hems dripping suns
eyes hurling miracles
she treads the raging thing as cloud
and snaps its skull like a locust shell!

Our apple dangles off the world
and rots between the fangs of hell . . . .

Pilgrim Song

A great sign appeared in heaven
a woman adorned with the sun
standing on the moon
and with twelve stars on her head
for a crown　　Revelation 12:1

When the world is an echo that lurks in the veins
whispering its ancient word
I cry the Inviolate's name to her hills
till Christ is the echo that's heard;

when lust is a lizard under the lids
waiting to spring on my sight
I stare the Inviolate out from her clouds
to blind me with torrents of light;

when the demon's a lover alone by my heart
and I grow aware of its charms
I pray the Inviolate down from her shrines
and bury my life in her arms!

REUNION

If we are children
we are heirs as well   Romans 8:17

Someday when all the worlds are old
and stories of God's love unfold

then all who share the vast reward
of life
of Lord

in that eternal Spring
shall throughout all Knowing
sing

how once a planet smiled
whose time had held His mother
whose race became His Child!